101 Things To Do With Chicken

101 Things To Do With Chicken

BY
DONNA KELLY AND
STEPHANIE ASHCRAFT

Gibbs Smith, Publisher
SALT LAKE CITY

First Edition
11 10 09 08 07   10 9 8 7 6 5 4 3 2 1

Published by
Gibbs Smith, Publisher
P.O. Box 667
Layton, Utah 84041

Orders: 1.800.835.4993
www.gibbs-smith.com

Designed by Kurt Wahlner
Printed and bound in Korea

Library of Congress Cataloging-in-Publication Data

Kelly, Donna.
  101 things to do with chicken / by Donna Kelly and Stephanie Ashcraft.—1st ed.
     p. cm.
  ISBN-13: 978-1-4236-0028-2
  1. Cookery (Chicken) I. Ashcraft, Stephanie. II. Title. III. Title: One hundred and one things to do with chicken.

TX750.5.C45K43 2007
641.6'65—dc22

2006020325

This book is dedicated to the Kelly kids—Katie, Amy, Matt and Jake—who have helped me to discover and rediscover the simple joys of everyday life, cooking included! —D.K.

To my sister, who gives me endless support and encouragement. To my "Avra Valley" family, who bless me and my family on a daily basis—thank you! And to my spouse and children, who bring me my greatest joy! —S.A.

CONTENTS

Company's Coming

Apple Cider Chicken 58 • Lemon Basil Chicken 59 • Garlic Lover's Roast Chicken 60 • Florentine Chicken Rolls 61 • Festive Chicken Crescent Wreath 62 • Gourmet Chicken Spirals 63 • Creamy Slow Cooker Chicken 64 • Apricot Pineapple Chicken Thighs 65 • Chicken Fajitas 66 • Cola Chicken 67 • Hawaiian Haystacks 68 • Cajun Chicken and Peppers 69 • Paprika Chicken 70

Main Dishes

Plum Good Chicken 72 • Balsamic Chicken Stacks 73 • Chicken Stir-Fry 74 • Almond-Crusted Chicken 75 • Lemonade Chicken 76 • Picante Chicken 77 • Bacon-Wrapped Chicken 78 • Chicken Cordon Bleu 79 • Cranberry Chicken and Rice 80 • Onion-Baked Chicken 81 • Mushroom-Stuffed Chicken Breasts 82 • Pecan-Crusted Chicken Breasts 83 • Sweet Hawaiian Chicken 84 • Chicken and Yam Bake 85

International Entrees

Tandoori Chicken 88 • Chicken Satay with Peanut Sauce 89 • Pastel de Choclo 90 • Canja Chicken Soup 91 • Kelaguen 92 • Chicken Enchilada Stacks 93 • Pomegranate Chicken 94 • Mediterranean Chicken 95 • Chicken Italiano 96 • 30-Minute Paella 97 • Asian Lettuce Wraps 98 • Chicken Yakisoba 99 • Jamaican Jerk Salad 100 • Chicken Stroganoff 101 • Chicken Curry 102

Family Favorites

BBQ Chicken Pizza 104 • Chicken Alfredo Pizza 105 • Breaded Chicken Nuggets 106 • Oven-Fried Buttermilk Chicken 107 • Parmesan-Crusted Drumsticks 108 • Family Fiesta Casserole 109 • One-Dish Sunday Supper 110 • Chicken Fajita Quesadillas 111 • Easy Chicken Picatta 112 • Chicken Broccoli Casserole 113 • Ranch-Seasoned Chicken 114 • Chicken Potpie 115 • Chicken and Sausage Cassoulet 116 • Mushroom and Artichoke Chicken 117 • Salsa Chicken 118 • Chicken and Rice Casserole 119 • Chicken Pastry Packets 120 • Grandma Dircks' Chicken Casserole 121

HELPFUL HINTS

1. Always make sure that chicken is thoroughly cooked. For chicken breasts, juices should run clear and the center should not be pink. Chicken thighs should reach 175 degrees when done. Never eat partially cooked chicken as salmonella may be present.

2. Wash your hands thoroughly with soap after handling raw chicken.

3. Always store chicken in the refrigerator or freezer until ready to use.

4. When purchasing chicken, check the sell by or use by dates. Make sure raw chicken is without blemish. For convenience, keep a bag of frozen chicken breasts handy for last-minute meals.

5. When recipes in this book call for boneless, skinless chicken breasts, this refers to either the chicken breast fillets that are frozen in bulk, or that can be purchased at your local grocery store's meat counter.

6. Place raw chicken in an airtight container when storing in the refrigerator to prevent juices from contaminating other foods. Raw chicken must be used within 1 or 2 days if stored in the refrigerator.

7. Frozen chicken should be defrosted before cooking. Defrost a whole frozen chicken for 36 hours in the refrigerator before using. Do not thaw chicken in a warm room where bacteria can breed. For chicken breasts or pieces, thaw 12 to 20 hours in the refrigerator before using.

8. Prepare raw chicken on a non-porous plastic cutting board that can be easily bleached or cleaned, and wash used cutting board at a high temperature.

9. To prevent cross-contamination, never use the same knife or measuring tool that was used to cut or touch raw chicken while preparing other ingredients.

10. Bring chicken to room temperature before cooking to ensure it will remain moist and will be cook evenly.

11. Leaving the skin on and the bone in the chicken while cooking will add flavor and moistness to the chicken. Whenever possible, do not pierce chicken pieces with a fork or knife while cooking—this allows the juices to run out and makes the chicken dry. Turn chicken pieces with a spoon or tongs while sauteing or frying.

12. Chicken is a very versatile and economical meat that can be cooked by many methods: broiling, grilling, roasting, sauteing, poaching, baking or slow cooking. White meat is leaner and more fragile than dark meat, so be careful not to overcook white meat when using dry methods, or it will become tough and rubbery.

13. Soaking chicken in brine will add flavor and moisture to baked or roasted chicken. Add $^1/_4$ cup salt to 1 quart of water and place chicken and brine in a ziplock bag. For a carmelized flavor that develops while cooking, also add $^1/_4$ cup sugar to the brine. Soak the chicken in the brine for at least 1 hour per pound, or overnight. Drain thoroughly before cooking.

14. For crispy skin when roasting or frying chicken, leave chicken uncovered in refrigerator for a few hours before cooking so the air will circulate and dry out the skin.

15. When roasting chicken or cooking by moist methods, allow chicken to stand at room temperature for about 10 minutes before slicing or serving so the moisture will be reabsorbed into the meat.

16. For planning recipes, remember that 1 pound of boneless, skinless chicken will yield about 3 cups of cubed or sliced chicken.

APPETIZERS

BBQ CHICKEN KABOBS

2 **boneless, skinless chicken breasts**
1 **red onion,** cut into 12 wedges
1 large **green bell pepper,** seeded and
cut into 12 pieces
1 large **red bell pepper,** seeded and
cut into 12 pieces
1 package (8 ounces) **fresh whole white mushrooms**
1 cup **barbecue sauce**

Preheat grill to high heat.

Cut each chicken breast into 6 pieces. Soften onion wedges in microwave
for 1 minute on high. Thread green bell pepper, onion wedge, chicken
piece, red bell pepper, and mushroom onto a skewer. Repeat with another
set of vegetables and chicken on the same skewer. Repeat the process
to fill 5 more skewers. Lightly brush some oil over the grill grate. Place
skewers on hot grill and then brush barbecue sauce over kabobs. Grill,
turning and brushing with additional sauce frequently, for 12–16 minutes,
or until chicken is done and vegetables are tender. Makes 6 servings.

BLUE CHEESE CHICKEN DIP

2 **boneless, skinless chicken
breasts,** cooked and shredded
1 $^1/_2$ cups **hot chicken wing sauce**
1 package (8 ounces) **cream cheese,** softened
1 bottle (16 ounces) **chunky blue cheese dressing**

Preheat oven to 350 degrees.

In a pan, combine shredded chicken and wing sauce. Bring to a boil
and reduce heat. Simmer over low heat for 8 minutes. Spread cream
cheese over bottom of a greased 8 x 8-inch pan. Pour chicken mixture
over cream cheese and then drizzle blue cheese dressing over top. Bake
15–18 minutes, or until bubbly. Serve with an assortment of tortilla
chips, crackers and pita triangles. Makes 10–12 servings.

FLAMING SOUTHWEST DIP

2 **boneless, skinless chicken breasts**
2 teaspoons **taco seasoning**
I package (8 ounces) **cream cheese,** softened
$^1/_2$ cup **mayonnaise**
$^1/_2$ cup **sour cream**
12 ounces **Velveeta cheese**, cubed
I can (4 ounces) **diced green chiles,** with liquid
I to 2 **jalapeno peppers,** seeded and chopped

Preheat oven to 350 degrees.

Place chicken on baking sheet. Lightly sprinkle taco seasoning over chicken and then bake 20 minutes, or until done in the center. Allow chicken to cool and then shred using two forks. Combine shredded chicken, cream cheese, mayonnaise, sour cream, Velveeta, chiles, and jalapenos in a greased 2-quart casserole dish. Bake, uncovered, for 25 minutes and then stir. Bake 10 minutes more, or until golden brown around edges. Serve with an assortment of crackers and tortilla chips. Makes 10–12 servings.

VARIATION: For a milder version, omit the jalapeno peppers.

nACHOS COn POLLO

1/2 cup **chopped green onions**
1 teaspoon **minced garlic**
3 tablespoons **olive oil**
1 can (10–13 ounces) **chunk chicken breast,** drained*
1 1/2 cups **chunky salsa**
1/2 bag (14-ounce size) **tortilla chips**
1 1/2 cups **grated Mexican blend cheese**

Preheat oven to 350 degrees.

In a skillet, saute green onions and garlic in oil until tender. Stir in chicken, shredding as you stir and completely coating it with oil. Mix in salsa. Place tortilla chips on bottom of a baking sheet. Spoon chicken mixture evenly over chips. Sprinkle cheese over top. Bake 10 minutes, or until cheese melts. Top with more fresh green onion if desired. Makes 8–10 servings.

*1 1/2 cups cooked and shredded chicken may be substituted.

BUFFALO WINGS

1 cup **Louisiana hot sauce** (cayenne pepper sauce)
1/2 cup **dark brown sugar**
1 cup **cornstarch**
1 teaspoon **salt**
18 (3 pounds) **chicken wings,** split and tips discarded

Mix hot sauce and brown sugar in a small bowl. Mix cornstarch and salt together and then spread on a small salad plate; dredge chicken in mixture until thoroughly coated. Dip chicken in hot sauce mixture until well coated. Place chicken wings on a broiling pan. Broil on high heat 8–10 minutes about 5–6 inches from the heat, watching closely so as not to burn chicken. Remove chicken from oven and turn pieces over. Brush with remaining sauce. Broil another 5–8 minutes, or until browned and cooked through. Serve with ranch or blue cheese dressing on the side for dipping. Makes 4–6 servings.

SWEET AND SPICY CHICKEN WINGS

18 (3 pounds)	**chicken wings,** split and tips discarded
$^1/_2$ cup	**soy sauce**
$^1/_2$ cup	**honey**
$^1/_4$ cup	**molasses**
2 tablespoons	**Tabasco sauce**
1 teaspoon	**ground ginger**
2 teaspoons	**minced garlic**

Place chicken in a 9 x 13-inch glass pan. In a bowl, combine remaining ingredients. Pour the mixture over the chicken. Cover and marinate overnight. Cook chicken over a hot grill basting with sauce mixture frequently, until juices run clear and chicken is done. Serve with ranch or blue cheese dressing on the side for dipping. Makes 6–8 servings.

VARIATION: Wings basted with sauce can also be baked for 45–50 minutes, or until done, at 375 degrees on a large baking sheet lined with aluminum foil. Turn halfway through baking and brush any remaining sauce over meat.

CHICKEN TOSTADA BITES

12	**thick gordita-style flour tortillas**
1 can (16 ounces)	**refried beans**
$^1/_2$ cup	**salsa**
2 cups	**grated cheddar cheese,** divided
2 cups	**cooked and diced chicken**
1 teaspoon	**salt**
1 teaspoon	**chipotle chili powder**
$^1/_2$ cup	**chopped cilantro**

Preheat oven to 400 degrees.

Using 2-inch-round cutters, cut circles out of tortillas. Place circles on a baking sheet and bake 5–8 minutes. Remove from oven and flatten circles with a kitchen towel. Turn circles over and bake 5–8 minutes more, or until crisped and lightly browned. Heat beans in a small saucepan. Stir in salsa and $^1/_2$ cup cheese; stir until melted. Toss chicken with salt and chili powder. To assemble, spread a thin layer of beans on tortilla circles. Top with a little chicken and cheese and then garnish with a sprinkle of cilantro. Makes 48 bites.

TANGY STRAWBERRY CHICKEN BITES

1 1/2 to 2 pounds **boneless, skinless chicken tender loins or breasts,** cut into small chunks

3 tablespoons **olive oil**

1 cup **strawberry preserves**

1 cup **chili sauce**

1 can (8 ounces) **pineapple chunks, drained**

Cook chicken chunks in oil over medium-high heat for 5–6 minutes, or until browned on all sides. Stir in preserves and chili sauce. Reduce heat to medium and simmer for 10 minutes. Stir the pineapple chunks into the skillet. Continue to simmer 2–3 minutes, or until pineapple is heated. Serve with toothpicks. Leftover sauce is also good over hot cooked vegetables or rice. Makes 10–12 servings.

COLD VEGETABLE PIZZA

1 tube (13.8 ounces)	**pizza crust dough**
1 cup	**prepared French onion dip**
1 1/2 to 2 cups	**chopped fresh broccoli**
1 1/4 cups	**cooked and cubed chicken**
1 medium	**tomato,** seeded and chopped
1/3 cup	**chopped green onions**

Preheat oven to 400 degrees.

Press out dough to cover a greased baking sheet. Bake 13 minutes, or until light golden brown. Allow crust to cool to room temperature. Spread dip over crust. Sprinkle broccoli, chicken, tomato, and green onions over pizza. Refrigerate until ready to serve. Cut into small squares. Makes 20–24 appetizers.

RANCH CHICKEN CHEESE BALL

2 packages (8 ounces each) **cream cheese,** softened
1 envelope **ranch dressing mix**
1 can (5 ounces) **chunk chicken breast,** drained
$^1/_3$ cup **chopped green onions**
$^2/_3$ cup **chopped pecans**

In a bowl, combine cream cheese, ranch dressing mix, chicken, and green onions. Spread pecans over a piece of wax paper. Form cream cheese mixture into a ball. Roll the ball in pecans until completely covered. Wrap in plastic wrap and chill for 1$^1/_2$ hours or overnight. Serve with an assortment of crackers. Makes 10–12 servings.

ROBYN'S ARTICHOKE SPREAD

2 cans (13.75 ounces each)	**artichoke hearts,** drained and chopped
1 cup	**grated Parmesan cheese**
1²/₃ cups	**light mayonnaise***
1 teaspoon	**garlic powder**
2 tablespoons	**chopped green onion**
1 to 2 cans (4 ounces each)	**diced green chiles**
1 can (10–13 ounces)	**white chicken breast meat,** drained

Preheat oven to 350 degrees.

In a bowl, combine all ingredients together. Spoon into a 1- to 2-quart casserole dish. Bake 35–45 minutes, uncovered, until brown and bubbly. Serve with crackers, tortilla chips or French bread.

*Light mayonnaise makes the spread less salty.

Soups & Salads

CHEESY BROCCOLI CHICKEN SOUP

2 cans (14 ounces each)	**chicken broth with garlic and herbs**
1 pound	**boneless, skinless chicken breasts,** cubed
1 pound	**fresh broccoli florets,** chopped
1/2 teaspoon	**black pepper**
1/3 cup	**butter**
1/3 cup	**flour**
1/2 cup	**heavy cream**
2 1/2 cups	**grated cheddar cheese**

In a stockpot, combine broth, chicken, broccoli, and pepper. Bring to a boil over high heat. Reduce heat and simmer over medium-low heat for 30–35 minutes.

In a saucepan, melt butter over medium heat. Mix in flour, stirring constantly until a thick paste forms. Remove from heat, and set aside. Stir the flour mixture into the pot a little at a time until soup thickens; simmer 5 minutes. Reduce heat, and stir in cream. Add cheese 1 cup at a time, stirring until melted. Serve in regular bowls or bread bowls. Makes 4–5 servings.

CHICKEN TACO SOUP

6 cups	**chicken broth**
4	**boneless, skinless chicken breasts,** cooked and cubed
I teaspoon	**cumin**
I tablespoon	**chipotle chili powder,** or more to taste
I can (29 ounces)	**crushed tomatoes in puree**
I can (I5 ounces)	**black beans,** drained
2 cups	**frozen corn**
I can (6 ounces)	**diced green chiles**
2 cups	**crushed tortilla chips**

In large pot, bring broth and chicken to a boil. Stir in remaining ingredients except chips and reduce heat to low. Simmer 50–60 minutes, stirring occasionally. Spoon soup into bowls and sprinkle crushed chips on top. Serve with optional garnish choices such as sour cream, grated cheddar cheese and chopped cilantro. Makes 6–8 servings.

WHITE LIGHTNING CHILI

I bag (16 ounces)	**dried white beans**
8 cups	**chicken broth**
$^1/_2$ cup	**diced green onions**
$^1/_2$ cup	**diced cilantro**
I can (4 ounces)	**diced green chiles,** mild or jalapeno
I tablespoon	**salt**
I teaspoon	**cumin**
2	**boneless, skinless chicken breasts,** finely diced

Cover beans with water and soak overnight. Drain and rinse beans.
Combine all ingredients and cook in a 3- to 4-quart slow cooker 3–4
hours on high heat, or 6–8 hours on low heat. Makes 4–6 servings.

VARIATION: For a quicker version, use canned white beans and simmer
all ingredients over medium to low heat on stovetop 30–40 minutes,
stirring frequently.

CHICKEN NOODLE SOUP

2 cans (14 ounces each)	**chicken broth**
2 cups	**water**
1/2	**yellow onion,** chopped
3	**carrots,** chopped
3 stalks	**celery,** chopped
1/2 teaspoon	**ground black pepper**
3 slices	**fresh gingerroot**
1 tablespoon	**olive oil**
1 cup	**chopped, cooked chicken breast**
1–2 cups	**uncooked egg noodles***

In a stockpot, combine broth, water, onion, carrots, celery and black pepper. Bring to a boil and then reduce to medium heat.

In a skillet, combine the gingerroot, oil and chicken. Saute over medium-high heat for about 5 minutes and then remove the ginger. Add the chicken to the broth mixture, bring to a boil and then add the noodles. Continue to cook over medium heat for about 15 minutes, or until the noodles and vegetables are tender. Makes 4 servings.

*Homemade egg noodles may take 5–10 minutes longer to cook.

CHICKEN AND DUMPLINGS

1 (4- to 5-pound)	**whole chicken,** cut up
1 teaspoon	**salt**
1 tablespoon	**Worcestershire sauce**
6 cups	**water**
1 cup	**chopped celery**
1 cup	**sliced carrots**
1 cup	**milk**
3 cups	**biscuit mix**
1 cup	**frozen peas**

In a large stockpot, bring chicken pieces, salt, Worcestershire sauce and water to a boil. Reduce heat to a simmer and cover and cook 20 minutes. Turn off heat and let sit for 1 hour. Place chicken pieces on a plate and when cool enough to handle, separate meat from skin and bones and cut into bite-size pieces. Return chicken to stockpot, and add celery and carrots. Cover and simmer 5 minutes. Meanwhile, stir milk into biscuit mix. Uncover soup and bring to a full boil. Stir in peas. Drop dough in golf ball–size chunks into boiling soup one at a time. Reduce heat and simmer about 10 minutes, or until dumplings are cooked through; serve hot. Makes 6–8 servings.

RANCH CHICKEN BEAN SOUP

5 cups	**water**
1 to 1 1/2 pounds	**boneless, skinless chicken breasts**
1 medium	**onion,** chopped
1 can (15 ounces)	**black beans,** drained and rinsed
2 cans (16 ounces each)	**dark kidney beans,** drained and rinsed
1 can (15 ounces)	**garbanzo beans,** drained and rinsed
2 cans (14.5 ounces each)	**diced tomatoes,** with liquid
1 envelope	**taco seasoning**
1 envelope	**ranch dressing mix**
	grated Mexican-blend cheese (optional)

In a 4- to 5-quart soup pan, combine water and chicken. Simmer over medium heat 30–45 minutes, or until chicken is thoroughly cooked. Remove chicken and cut into bite-size pieces. Return chicken to the broth and stir in onion, beans, tomatoes, taco seasoning and ranch dressing mix. Simmer 20 minutes over medium-low heat until heated through. Garnish with cheese, if desired. Makes 8–10 servings.

CHICKEN CORN CHOWDER

4 slices	**bacon**
I cup	**diced celery**
$^1/_2$ cup	**minced onion**
$^1/_2$ cup	**minced carrots**
$^1/_4$ cup	**flour**
I can (32 ounces)	**chicken broth**
2	**boneless, skinless chicken breasts,** cut into bite-size pieces
I bag (16 ounces)	**frozen corn**
I cup	**whipping cream** **salt and pepper**

In large stockpot, cook bacon over medium-high heat until crisp. Drain excess fat, leaving about 3 tablespoons in the pan. Add celery, onion and carrots and saute for 3 minutes, or until limp. Stir in flour until vegetables are evenly coated; add broth and stir. Add chicken and corn. Bring to a boil and then reduce heat to medium and simmer for 20 minutes. Stir in cream and simmer 3–5 minutes more. Add salt and pepper to taste. Makes 6–8 servings.

SOUTHWEST CHICKEN SOUP

2	**boneless, skinless chicken breasts,** diced
I tablespoon	**butter**
¹/2 medium	**onion,** chopped
I whole	**Anaheim chile,** seeded and chopped
I tablespoon	**minced garlic**
3 cups	**chicken broth**
I can (14 ounces)	**red enchilada sauce**
4	**corn tortillas**
2 cups	**grated cheddar cheese**
I cup	**sour cream**
¹/2 cup	**chopped cilantro** (optional)

Saute chicken in butter in a large saucepan. Add onion, chile and garlic and cook until tender. Add broth and enchilada sauce. Cut tortillas into thin strips, about ¹/4 x 3 inches and then add to soup. Add cheese and simmer 5–10 minutes, or until soup thickens slightly. Turn off heat, stir in sour cream and serve. Garnish with chopped cilantro, if desired. Makes 4–6 servings.

VARIATION: Replace the Anaheim chile with I can (4 ounces) diced green chiles, mild or jalapeno.

POTATO CHICKEN CHOWDER

I cup	**diced ham**
I pound	**boneless, skinless chicken breasts,** diced
2 tablespoons	**butter**
I large	**onion,** chopped
3 medium	**potatoes,** peeled and cubed
3 cups	**chicken broth**
2 cups	**milk**
I cup	**heavy cream**
2 tablespoons	**minced parsley**
	salt and pepper, to taste

In a frying pan, saute ham, chicken and onion in butter until onion is limp. Add potatoes and saute for 15 minutes, stirring constantly. Add broth and milk; bring to a boil. Reduce heat and simmer for 30 minutes. Stir in cream and parsley. Salt and pepper to taste. Simmer 5 minutes more. Serve in regular bowls or bread bowls. Makes 4–6 servings.

SWEET AND SOUR ALMOND SALAD

1 package (3 ounces) **ramen noodles**
$^1/_4$ cup **butter**
1 cup **slivered almonds**
1 pound **fresh broccoli florets**
1 head **romaine lettuce,** washed and torn
1 $^1/_2$ cups **cooked, cubed chicken**
$^1/_3$ cup **chopped green onions**

Dressing:
$^1/_2$ cup **vegetable oil**
$^1/_4$ cup **sugar**
$^1/_4$ cup **apple cider vinegar**
1 $^1/_2$ tablespoons **soy sauce**
$^1/_4$ teaspoon **black pepper**

Discard or save seasoning packet from ramen noodles for another use. Melt butter in skillet. Break dry noodles into small pieces and fry dry noodles and almonds in melted butter until lightly toasted.

In a large bowl, toss together cooled noodle mixture, broccoli, lettuce, chicken, and green onions. Mix all dressing ingredients together and refrigerate until ready to serve. Just before serving, add $^1/_2$ cup dressing and toss the salad to coat. Serve with remaining dressing on the side to be added as desired. Makes 6–8 servings.

SUMMER CHICKEN SALAD

3	**boneless, skinless chicken breasts,** cooked and cubed
I large head	**dark leaf lettuce**
I cup	**raspberry vinaigrette**
$^1/_2$ cup	**vanilla yogurt**
I cup	**thinly sliced celery**
2 cups	**sliced fresh strawberries**
I cup	**honey roasted sliced almonds or peanuts**

Chill chicken in refrigerator at least 30 minutes. Chop lettuce and place in a large serving bowl. Add chilled chicken pieces. Stir vinaigrette and yogurt together until smooth. Pour over lettuce and chicken and toss. Sprinkle on celery, strawberries and nuts. Makes 6–8 servings.

WINTER CHICKEN SALAD

    3 **boneless, skinless chicken breasts,**
        cooked and cubed
    1 **Granny Smith or Gala apple,** chopped
 $1/2$ cup **chopped celery**
 $1/2$ cup **dried sweetened cranberries**
 $1/2$ cup **chopped walnuts**
 $1/2$ cup **vanilla yogurt**
 1 teaspoon **lemon juice**
 1 teaspoon **sugar**

Chill chicken in refrigerator at least 30 minutes. Combine chicken, apple, celery, dried cranberries, and nuts in a medium bowl. Mix remaining ingredients and pour into bowl. Add chilled chicken and stir. Serve chilled over a lettuce leaf or use as a filling for sandwiches. Makes 6–8 servings.

CHOPPED FIESTA SALAD

2 cans (16 ounces each)	**black beans,** drained and rinsed
1 bag (16 ounces)	**frozen corn,** thawed
2 large	**tomatoes,** chopped
2	**green bell peppers,** chopped
1 cup	**zesty Italian salad dressing**
3	**chicken breasts,** cooked and chopped into small cubes
1 teaspoon	**seasoned salt**
2 cans (7 ounces each)	**sliced black olives**

In a 2-quart glass trifle bowl, layer the beans, corn, tomatoes and bell peppers. Pour the dressing over top. Season chicken with seasoned salt and spread on top. Sprinkle olives over the chicken and then cover with plastic wrap and chill 2 hours or overnight. Serve chilled. Makes 6 servings.

CHICKEN CAESAR SALAD

$^3/_4$ to 1 pound **frozen breaded chicken breast strips or fillets**
1 head **romaine lettuce,** washed and torn
$^1/_2$ **red onion,** thinly sliced
$^1/_3$ cup **grated Parmesan cheese**
1 cup **Caesar dressing**
1 cup **croutons**

Bake or fry chicken strips or fillets according to package directions until crispy. Slice cooked chicken.

In a large bowl, combine lettuce, onion, Parmesan cheese, dressing, and croutons. Toss until coated with dressing. Lay chicken slices over top and serve immediately. Makes 6–8 servings.

CURRIED CHICKEN SALAD

3 cups	**cooked cubed chicken**
1 can (8 ounces)	**sliced water chestnuts,** drained
1 can (11 ounces)	**mandarin oranges,** drained
$^3/_4$ cup	**mayonnaise**
1 teaspoon	**curry powder**
1 $^1/_2$ teaspoons	**soy sauce**
1 $^1/_2$ teaspoons	**lemon juice**
1 bag (10 ounces)	**romaine lettuce**

Combine chicken, water chestnuts, and oranges; set aside.

In a bowl, combine mayonnaise, curry, soy sauce, and lemon juice. Add dressing to chicken mixture. Chill until ready to serve. Serve on beds of romaine lettuce. Makes 6 servings.

CHICKEN AND RICE SALAD

2	**boneless, skinless chicken breasts** cooked and finely diced
3 cups	**cooked rice**
I cup	**frozen peas,** thawed
I cup	**diced celery**
$^1/_2$	**red bell pepper,** diced
I cup	**toasted sliced almonds**
3	**green onions,** thinly sliced
I can (8 ounces)	**pineapple tidbits,** with juice
I cup	**Italian dressing**
$^1/_2$ cup	**toasted sesame seeds,** divided

Combine all ingredients except dressing and sesame seeds in a medium-size serving bowl. Refrigerate 2 hours or overnight. Toss with dressing and $^1/_4$ cup sesame seeds. Sprinkle remaining sesame seeds on top as a garnish. Makes 8–10 servings.

MEDITERRANEAN CHICKEN SALAD

2 1/2 cups	**cooked and cubed chicken**
1	**carrot,** peeled and sliced
1	**cucumber,** sliced
1 can (2.25 ounces)	**sliced black olives,** drained
4 ounces	**crumbled feta cheese**
1/2 cup	**Greek salad dressing**

In a large bowl, toss chicken, carrot, cucumber, olives, and cheese. Gently stir in salad dressing. Cover and refrigerate for at least 1 hour. Add more dressing if desired. Makes 4–6 servings.

VARIATION: Cubed raw chicken can be cooked in 1/4 cup Greek salad dressing for additional flavor.

BOWTIE PASTA SALAD

1 package (16 ounces) **bowtie pasta**
$1/4$ cup **sesame oil**
$1/4$ cup **canola oil**
$1/3$ cup **white vinegar**
$1/2$ cup **soy sauce**
4 tablespoons **sugar**
3 **boneless, skinless chicken breasts,** cooked and cubed
1 large **bunch spinach,** chopped
1 can (11 ounces) **mandarin oranges,** drained
1 can (8 ounces) **pineapple tidbits,** drained
2 cups **grapes,** halved
$1/2$ cup **sliced almonds**
$1/4$ cup **toasted sesame seeds**

Boil pasta to al dente stage according to package directions; rinse and cool. Mix together oils, vinegar, soy sauce and sugar. Toss pasta with sauce mixture and chill in refrigerator for up to 2 hours, or until well chilled.

In large serving bowl, toss pasta, chicken, spinach, oranges, pineapple, grapes and almonds. Sprinkle sesame seeds on top and serve immediately. Makes 8–10 servings.

Sandwiches & Wraps

NUTTY PINEAPPLE CHICKEN SANDWICHES

I package (8 ounces)	**cream cheese,** softened
I can (8 ounces)	**crushed pineapple,** drained
$1/2$ cup	**finely chopped pecans**
12 slices	**raisin bread**
12 slices	**deli chicken sandwich meat**
6	**dark lettuce leaves**

Mix cream cheese, pineapple and nuts. Lightly toast bread and let cool. Spread all slices of bread with a thick layer of the cream cheese mixture. Place 2 slices of meat on half the bread slices. Place a lettuce leaf on top of chicken and then top with remaining bread slices. Makes 6 sandwiches.

GRILLED SWISS SANDWICHES

2 tablespoons	**sour cream***
4	**slices bread,** any variety
4 slices	**Swiss cheese**
2 slices	**deli chicken sandwich meat**
2 slices	**deli ham**
2 tablespoons	**butter,** softened

Spread $^1/_2$ tablespoon sour cream on one side of each bread slice. Over two pieces of bread, layer one slice of cheese, one slice of chicken, one slice of ham, and another slice of cheese. Place the remaining two pieces of bread, sour cream side down, to top sandwiches. Lightly spread softened butter over both sides of each sandwich. Grill sandwiches until cheese melts and bread is toasted. Makes 2 servings.

*Ranch dip or French onion dip can be used in place of sour cream.

ZESTY CHICKEN BURGERS

3 **boneless, skinless chicken breasts***
$1/2$ **red bell pepper,** chopped
$1/2$ cup **loosely packed chopped cilantro**
$1/2$ cup **chopped green onions**
$1/2$ cup **chili sauce** (or cocktail sauce)
I teaspoon **salt**
8 **hamburger buns**

Cut chicken into large chunks and then process in a food processor until coarsely ground. Place in medium mixing bowl. Process bell pepper, cilantro and onions in a food processor until finely diced. Mix into bowl with chicken. Add chili sauce and salt and stir until blended. Form into 8 patties, about $1/2$ inch thick. Coat broiling pan or outdoor grill with oil or nonstick cooking spray. Broil or grill patties over high heat for 10–12 minutes on first side. Turn over and broil or grill 6–8 minutes on other side. Serve hot on buns with traditional burger condiments. Makes 8 servings.

*If you don't have a food processor available, substitute I $1/2$ pounds ground chicken and mix with remaining ingredients.

GRILLED HONEY MUSTARD CHICKEN SANDWICHES

4 **boneless, skinless chicken breasts**
I can (20 ounces) **sliced pineapple,** drained
$^2/_3$ cup **honey mustard**
4 **large buns**
$^1/_2$ **medium red onion,** thinly sliced

Grill chicken breasts and pineapple slices, frequently brushing both with honey mustard, until chicken is thoroughly cooked. Serve on buns topped with grilled pineapple, onion, and additional honey mustard. Makes 4 servings.

PULLED CHICKEN SANDWICHES

1 (3 1/2- to 4-pound) **whole chicken,** cut up
3/4 cup **apple cider vinegar**
1/4 cup **brown sugar**
1 teaspoon **salt**
1 teaspoon **pepper**
2 cups **ketchup**
3/4 cup **honey**
1 dash **Worcestershire sauce**
8 large **buns**

Place whole chicken in a 3- to 4-quart slow cooker and cook 6–8 hours on low heat. (Or, place whole chicken in a covered roasting pan and cook 6 hours in oven at 275 degrees.)

In a small saucepan, bring vinegar to a rapid boil and then turn off heat. Add remaining ingredients to saucepan, while stirring. Remove chicken from slow cooker or oven. While chicken is still hot, use two forks to pull meat off bones and place in a small baking dish. Stir in half the sauce and then let chicken stand about 10 minutes to absorb sauce and to cool off slightly. Serve on buns with remaining sauce on the side. Makes 6–8 servings.

VARIATION: To make things even easier, skip the slow cooker step and use a rotisserie chicken from the grocery store and your favorite bottle of barbecue sauce.

BBQ BACON CHICKEN BURGER

4	**boneless, skinless chicken breasts**
I jar (18 ounces)	**barbecue sauce,** divided
4 slices	**Swiss cheese**
4	**hamburger buns**
8 slices	**cooked bacon**

Marinate chicken in two-thirds of the barbecue sauce for 4 hours or overnight in the refrigerator. Grill marinated chicken on a hot grill, basting with new barbecue sauce until juices run clear and chicken is done. Lay slice of cheese over each chicken breast to melt. Serve chicken breasts on warm buns with bacon and favorite toppings. Makes 4 servings.

CHICKEN PARMESAN SUBS

4 **breaded boneless, skinless chicken breasts**
2 cups **spaghetti sauce**
4 **submarine rolls**
1 cup **grated mozzarella cheese**

Bake or fry breaded chicken according to package directions. Heat spaghetti sauce in a saucepan. When chicken is done, place a chicken breast onto a toasted submarine roll. Spoon warm spaghetti sauce over chicken. Sprinkle $1/4$ cup cheese over sauce. Serve immediately with remaining warm sauce for dipping. Makes 4 servings.

ITALIAN CHICKEN SUBS

4	**boneless, skinless chicken breasts**
1 bottle (16 ounces)	**Italian salad dressing**
4	**submarine rolls**
	mayonnaise
	sliced red onion
	sliced tomato

Marinate chicken breasts in Italian dressing for 4 hours or overnight. Grill chicken breast until juices run clear and it is no longer pink in the center. Serve on warm buns with mayonnaise, onion, and tomato or other favorite sandwich toppings. Makes 4 servings.

CHICKEN CAESAR WRAPS

2 **boneless, skinless chicken breasts,** cooked, cut into thin strips and chilled

I small head **romaine lettuce**

$^1/_2$ cup **Caesar salad dressing**

$^1/_4$ cup **grated Parmesan cheese**

$^1/_2$ **medium red onion,** thinly sliced

4 **large burrito-size tortillas**

Combine chicken, lettuce, dressing, cheese, and onion. Spoon evenly over tortillas and roll up. Makes 4 servings.

CRANBERRY CHICKEN SPINACH WRAPS

1 cup	**mayonnaise**
1 envelope	**ranch dressing mix**
6 large	**burrito-size tortillas**
1 package (16 ounces)	**shaved deli chicken breast slices**
1 bag (6 ounces)	**dried cranberries**
1 bag (6 ounces)	**spinach leaves**
1 cup	**grated sharp cheddar cheese**

Stir together mayonnaise and ranch dressing mix. Spread a layer of mayonnaise mixture evenly over each tortilla. Place chicken slices over top. Sprinkle 1 ounce dried cranberries down center of tortilla. Layer spinach leaves on half the tortilla. Sprinkle 2 tablespoons cheese over spinach. Roll starting with the spinach side and then wrap in plastic wrap and chill until ready to serve. Repeat the process for remaining tortillas. Makes 6 servings.

VARIATION: Can be made the night before serving. One container (8 ounces) plain yogurt may be used in place of mayonnaise.

CHICKEN SALAD WRAPS

1 can (10–13 ounces) **white chicken breast meat,** drained
1/3 cup **mayonnaise**
1/4 cup **cashew halves**
1 cup **seedless red grape halves**
2 **burrito-size flour tortillas**
1 cup **washed, torn lettuce**

Combine chicken, mayonnaise, cashews, and grapes. Evenly divide and spread chicken mixture down center of each tortilla. Lay lettuce over chicken mixture. Roll each tortilla burrito style. Makes 2 servings.

CALIFORNIA WRAPS

4 **boneless, skinless chicken breasts,** cut into strips
2 tablespoons **olive oil**
$^1/_2$ cup **ranch dressing**
4 **burrito-size flour tortillas**
1 **avocado,** peeled and cubed
2 tablespoons **lime juice**
1$^1/_2$ cups **torn lettuce**
1 **medium tomato,** chopped
$^1/_2$ cup **crumbled cooked bacon pieces**

Cook chicken strips in oil until juices run clear and then chill chicken. Stir dressing into chilled chicken. Equally divide the ranch chicken and spread down the center of each tortilla. Toss avocado cubes with lime juice. Sprinkle lettuce, tomato, avocado, and bacon evenly over each tortilla. Roll each tortilla burrito style. Makes 4 servings.

Company's Coming

APPLE CIDER CHICKEN

I (5- to 6-pound) **whole chicken,** at room temperature
I tablespoon **salt**
4 cups **clear apple cider**
$^1/_4$ cup **melted butter**

Place chicken in a gallon-size ziplock bag. Stir salt into cider, pour over chicken and then seal bag. Put bag in a pan and refrigerate 12–24 hours, turning over occasionally. Remove chicken and drain cider into a small saucepan. Pat chicken dry and then brush with melted butter. Place chicken into a covered roasting pan and bake for 50–60 minutes at 375 degrees. Meanwhile, bring the reserved cider to a boil in a small saucepan. Turn heat down and simmer until reduced to I cup. Remove chicken from oven and carefully remove skin. Return to oven, uncovered, and bake another 30 minutes, basting every I0 minutes with reduced cider. Remove from oven, turn chicken breast side down and let stand I0 minutes before serving. Makes 6–8 servings.

LEMON BASIL CHICKEN

1 (4- to 5-pound) **whole chicken,** at room temperature
1 large **bunch fresh basil leaves**
2 **whole lemons**
3/4 cup **olive oil**
1 teaspoon **salt**

Carefully separate skin from chicken with fingers without removing skin. Place about 8 basil leaves under chicken skin. Cut one lemon into very thin slices and place 4 slices under skin on top of basil leaves. Cut remaining lemon into four wedges and squeeze juice into blender. Add 1/2 cup oil, salt and remaining basil leaves to blender and blend. Spoon 3 tablespoons basil mixture into cavity of chicken. Place lemon wedges into cavity of chicken. Refrigerate 4 hours or overnight. Bring chicken to room temperature and then place in a covered roasting pan. Bake at 375 degrees for 30 minutes. Remove chicken from oven and brush remaining basil mixture onto chicken. Return to oven and bake, uncovered, another 30–50 minutes, or until chicken is golden brown and done. Remove from oven, turn chicken breast side down and let stand 10 minutes before serving. Makes 6–8 servings.

GARLIC LOVER'S ROAST CHICKEN

1 jar (4 ounces) **crushed garlic puree**
2 tablespoons **butter,** softened
1 teaspoon **salt**
1 (4- to 5-pound) **whole chicken,** at room temperature

Preheat oven to 375 degrees.

Stir together garlic, butter and salt. With fingers, loosen chicken skin above breast and spread one-third of garlic mixture under skin, and then another one-third in chicken cavity. Truss chicken with string or bamboo skewer. Rub remaining garlic mixture on outside of chicken. Place chicken in covered roasting pan and bake in oven for 60 minutes, breast side up. Remove from oven, increase heat to 425 degrees and baste chicken with drippings from bottom of pan. Bake, uncovered, another 10 minutes, or until well browned. Remove from oven and let stand 10 minutes before carving. Makes 8 servings.

FLORENTINE CHICKEN ROLLS

1 cup **ricotta cheese**
$^1/_2$ cup **grated Parmesan cheese**
1 teaspoon **garlic salt**
1 box (10 ounces) **frozen chopped spinach,** thawed
and drained
2 **eggs**
6 **boneless, skinless chicken breasts**

Preheat oven to 350 degrees.

Combine all ingredients except chicken in a small bowl and set aside.
Place each breast between sheets of plastic wrap and pound to $^1/_2$ inch
thickness. Spread $^1/_2$ cup of the spinach mixture on each flattened
breast and then roll up breast, securing with a long toothpick. Place
breast rolls in a 9 x 13-inch pan, seam side down, and then cover with
foil. Bake for 30 minutes. Uncover and bake another 15–20 minutes, or
until browned. Remove chicken rolls and place on a platter. Pour a little
water into pan and scrape with a wooden spoon to deglaze pan. Pour
pan juices on top of chicken rolls and serve while still warm. Makes
6 servings.

FESTIVE CHICKEN CRESCENT WREATH

2 tubes (10 ounces each) **ready-to-bake crescent rolls**
2 cups **grated pepper jack cheese**
$^1/_2$ cup **sour cream**
1 cup **diced fresh broccoli**
$^1/_2$ cup **diced red bell pepper**
$^1/_4$ cup **diced green onions**
1 can (10 ounces) **white chicken,** drained

Preheat oven to 375 degrees.

Unroll crescent rolls and arrange on a 15-inch-round pizza pan, with wide edges of dough triangles about 2 inches in from outside edge of pan and pointed edges hanging off the pan. Wide edges of dough triangles should overlap about 2 inches. Mix remaining ingredients and spoon onto top of wide edges of dough circle, all the way around the circle. Bring pointed edges of dough up and fold over the chicken mixture and tuck into inside of the circle. Some filling will be showing between each section of dough. Bake for 20–25 minutes, or until golden brown. Makes 6–8 servings.

GOURMET CHICKEN SPIRALS

I jar (8 ounces) **sun-dried tomatoes in oil**
I cup **finely diced fresh basil or spinach**
6 ounces **goat cheese or cream cheese**
3 **boneless, skinless chicken breasts,** partially frozen
I envelope (0.7 ounces) **Italian salad dressing mix**
$^1/_2$ cup **water**

Preheat oven to 350 degrees.

Dice tomatoes and mix with oil, basil and goat cheese. Place chicken breasts on cutting board, and with a large sharp knife parallel to cutting board, cut breasts in half so there are two large flat planks from each breast. Place breasts between two sheets of plastic wrap and pound to $^1/_4$ inch thickness. Spread $^1/_4$ cup tomato mixture on each flattened breast piece. Roll up, jelly-roll style. Cut chicken into 2-inch pieces, slicing so that spiral filling shows and secure with long toothpick. Place spiral side up in a 9 x 13-inch baking pan. Sprinkle each spiral with dry dressing mix. Bake, uncovered, for 30–40 minutes, or until browned. Remove spirals from pan and place on serving platter. Pour water into pan and stir with a wooden spoon to deglaze pan. Pour juices over spirals and serve warm. Makes 6 servings.

CREAMY SLOW COOKER CHICKEN

8	**boneless, skinless chicken breasts**
$^1/_2$ cup	**butter,** melted
2 envelopes (0.7 ounces each)	**Italian salad dressing mix**
1 package (8 ounces)	**cream cheese,** softened
8 cups	**cooked rice**

Dip chicken in butter and then sprinkle generously with dry dressing mix. Place chicken in a 6- to 7-quart slow cooker. Mix any remaining butter and dry mix and pour over chicken. Cover and cook 3–4 hours on high heat or 6–8 hours on low heat. Remove chicken and stir cream cheese into liquid in slow cooker. Add water if necessary to make the consistency of gravy. Return chicken pieces and cook another 30 minutes on high heat. Serve chicken with sauce over rice. Makes 8 servings.

APRICOT PINEAPPLE CHICKEN THIGHS

I cup	**apricot pineapple jam**
I teaspoon	**garlic powder**
I tablespoon	**Worcestershire sauce**
I teaspoon	**salt**
$2^1/_2$ to 3 pounds	**skinless chicken thighs**

Preheat oven to 375 degrees.

Mix all ingredients together except chicken. Brush chicken thighs with mixture, then place in a 2-quart baking dish. Pour remaining sauce over top. Bake for 40–50 minutes, or until cooked through. Remove from oven and let sit 5 minutes before serving. Makes 4–6 servings.

CHICKEN FAJITAS

3 pounds	**boneless, skinless chicken breasts**
1 teaspoon	**cumin**
1 teaspoon	**salt**
2 teaspoons	**chipotle chili powder**
$1/4$ cup	**lime juice**
2 large	**red onions**
2	**each green and red bell peppers**
8 to 10	**medium-size flour tortillas**

Slice chicken lengthwise into $1/4$-inch strips and then place in a 5- to 7-quart slow cooker. Mix cumin, salt, chili powder and lime juice and stir into chicken. Cut onions and peppers into large julienne strips and place on top of chicken. Cover and cook 3–4 hours on low heat. Remove cover and stir; cook on high 1 more hour, allowing liquid to evaporate. Serve with warm flour tortillas. Makes 8–10 servings.

COLA CHICKEN

2 large **yellow onions**
3 to 4 pounds **chicken pieces**
1 can (12 ounces) **cola soda** (not diet)
2 cups **ketchup**

Preheat oven to 350 degrees.

Slice onions into $1/2$-inch-thick slices and spread in a 9 x 13-inch baking pan. Place chicken pieces on top. Mix cola and ketchup together and then pour over top. Cover with foil and bake for 1 hour. Uncover and bake another 20–30 minutes, or until chicken is golden brown. Makes 6–8 servings.

HAWAIIAN HAYSTACKS

1 (4- to 5-pound)	**whole cooked rotisserie chicken**
$^{1}/_{2}$ cup	**flour**
4 cups	**chicken broth**
2 cups	**chopped green bell pepper**
2 cups	**chopped celery**
2 cups	**chopped carrots**
8 cups	**cooked rice**
1 bag (12 ounces)	**chow mein noodles**
1 cup	**diced green onions**
2 cans (8 ounces each)	**sliced water chestnuts**
2 cans (16 ounces each)	**pineapple tidbits,** drained
$^{1}/_{2}$ cup	**toasted coconut**
1 cup	**sliced toasted almonds or cashews**

Remove chicken from bones and cut into bite-size pieces. Mix flour with a little water and then stir into broth and simmer in a medium saucepan until thickened to make the gravy. Microwave bell pepper, celery and carrots until cooked through but still firm. Place all ingredients in separate bowls and have each person make their own "haystack," layering food in the following order: rice, chicken, gravy, chow mein noodles, vegetables, pineapple, coconut, nuts. Makes 8–10 servings.

CAJUN CHICKEN AND PEPPERS

2 tablespoons	**canola oil**
1 tablespoon	**butter**
8	**skinless chicken thighs**
8 tablespoons	**Worcestershire sauce**
8 teaspoons	**Cajun spice**
1	**red bell pepper,** julienned
1	**green bell pepper,** julienned
1 large	**red onion,** julienned
1 cup	**water**
8 cups	**cooked rice**

Preheat oven to 375 degrees.

Heat the oil and butter in a large skillet. Coat each chicken thigh with
1 tablespoon Worcestershire sauce and 1 teaspoon Cajun spice. Saute
thighs for 5 minutes, turning once. Place bell peppers and onion into a
2-quart casserole dish. Place thighs on top. Stir water into skillet over
high heat to deglaze pan. Pour liquid over top of thighs. Cover and
bake for 30–40 minutes, or until vegetables are cooked through. Serve
with rice. Makes 6–8 servings.

PAPRIKA CHICKEN

4 tablespoons	**canola oil**
1 tablespoon	**butter**
2 to 3 pounds	**boneless, skinless chicken pieces**
1	**large onion,** diced
1 can (14 ounces)	**chicken broth**
3 tablespoons	**paprika**
2 teaspoons	**flour**
12 ounces	**regular or light sour cream**

Heat oil and butter in a large skillet. Brown the chicken pieces in skillet a few at a time, about 2 minutes on each side. Remove chicken and place in a large oven-proof serving dish; keep warm in oven. Add onions to skillet and saute 2–3 minutes, or until limp. Add broth and paprika. Bring to a boil and then reduce to a simmer. Cook, uncovered, for 30 minutes, or until reduced by half. Mix flour into sour cream with a fork. Whisk the sour cream mixture into the skillet and cook until bubbly. Remove chicken from oven and pour sauce over top. Serve with noodles, mashed potatoes or rice. Makes 4–6 servings.

MAIN DISHES

PLUM GOOD CHICKEN

4 to 5 pounds	**chicken thighs** (about 12 thighs)
I can (12 ounces)	**frozen lemonade concentrate,** thawed
3 tablespoons	**canola oil**
I tablespoon	**minced garlic**
I tablespoon	**minced ginger**
1/3 cup	**plum sauce**
3 tablespoons	**tomato paste**
3 tablespoons	**soy sauce**

Remove skin and visible fat from chicken and place in a gallon-size ziplock bag. Add lemonade concentrate to bag and refrigerate 2–4 hours. Remove from refrigerator and bring to room temperature. Drain marinade, reserving 2/3 cup. Preheat oven to 350 degrees.

Heat oil in a medium frying pan. Saute chicken over medium-high heat a few pieces at a time for about 2 minutes on each side, or until browned. Place chicken in a 9 x 13-inch baking pan. Add the reserved lemonade marinade and the remaining ingredients to a small saucepan and simmer for a few minutes, thickening slightly. Pour over chicken and then bake 40 minutes. Serve with sauce over rice. Makes 4–6 servings.

BALSAMIC CHICKEN STACKS

3 **partially frozen chicken breasts**
$^1/_2$ cup **balsamic vinegar**
$^1/_4$ cup **soy sauce**
$^1/_4$ cup **honey**
2 pounds **fresh spinach,** coarsely chopped
16 ounces **sliced mushrooms**
2 tablespoons **butter**
1 teaspoon **garlic powder**
6 cups **cooked rice**

Lay breasts flat and, with knife parallel to cutting surface, cut breasts into two large flat planks. Mix vinegar, soy sauce and honey. Brush this over chicken pieces and then broil for 6–8 minutes on each side, or until golden brown. Remove chicken from oven and brush with sauce again and then let stand a few minutes. Pour remaining sauce in a large skillet or wok. Place spinach on top and cover. Cook on high heat, stirring until spinach is cooked down. Saute mushrooms in butter for a few minutes and sprinkle with garlic powder in a small frying pan. On each serving plate, make a stack as follows: $^1/_2$ cup rice, $^1/_2$ cup spinach, 1 chicken piece, and $^1/_2$ cup sauteed mushrooms. Makes 6 servings.

CHICKEN STIR-FRY

2 pounds	**boneless, skinless dark chicken meat**
3 tablespoons	**soy sauce**
I teaspoon	**garlic powder**
$1/4$ cup	**cornstarch**
$1/4$ cup	**canola oil**
8 cups	**chopped fresh vegetables,** such as broccoli, carrots and celery
I jar (I2 ounces)	**stir-fry sauce**
$1/2$ cup	**water**
6 cups	**cooked rice**

Chop chicken and place in a gallon-size ziplock bag. Mix together soy sauce, garlic powder and cornstarch and then pour into ziplock bag. Set aside at room temperature, turning frequently, up to 30 minutes. Heat oil in wok or large frying pan. Add vegetables and stir fry for a few minutes, or until slightly softened but not done; add chicken. Cook another few minutes. Add stir-fry sauce and water. Cook until heated through and chicken is no longer pink. If sauce is not thickened to your liking, mix a little cornstarch and water and stir into mixture, cooking until thickened. Serve over rice. Makes 6–8 servings.

GARLIC CHICKEN VARIATION: After oil is heated, stir in 2 to 3 tablespoons minced fresh garlic and cook until lightly browned. Add remaining ingredients, omitting stir-fry sauce and adding $1/2$ cup water.

GINGER CHICKEN VARIATION: After oil is heated, add 2 to 3 tablespoons grated fresh ginger and cook until limp. Add remaining ingredients, omitting stir-fry sauce and adding $1/2$ cup water.

ALMOND-CRUSTED CHICKEN

5	**boneless, skinless chicken breasts**
I bottle (16 ounces)	**Italian salad dressing**
I cup	**slivered almonds**
5 ounces	**grated Asiago cheese**

Marinate chicken in salad dressing overnight. Preheat oven to 375 degrees.

In a food processor or blender, chop almonds and Asiago cheese together. Place mixture in a bowl. Roll chicken in mixture and place on bottom of a greased 9 x 13-inch pan. Cover with aluminum foil and bake for 25 minutes. Uncover and bake an additional 15–20 minutes, or until done. Makes 5 servings.

LEMONADE CHICKEN

6	**boneless, skinless chicken breasts**
I small can (6 ounces)	**frozen lemonade**
$^1/_4$ cup	**soy sauce**
I teaspoon	**garlic powder**

Preheat oven to 375 degrees.

Slice chicken breasts in half lengthwise and place in a gallon-size ziplock bag. Combine lemonade, soy sauce and garlic powder and pour over chicken. Refrigerate 2–4 hours, or more. (The longer the chicken marinates, the stronger the lemon flavor becomes.) Remove chicken from refrigerator and bring to room temperature, about 20–30 minutes. Place in a 9 x 13-inch pan and bake for 45–60 minutes, turning chicken and basting every 10–15 minutes, or until golden brown. Let stand 5 minutes before serving. Makes 6 servings.

PICANTE CHICKEN

6	**boneless, skinless chicken breasts**
$^1/_4$ cup	**hot pepper jelly**
2 tablespoons	**red wine or apple cider vinegar**
2 teaspoons	**Dijon mustard**
I teaspoon	**salt**

Place chicken breasts between two sheets of plastic wrap and pound to $^1/_2$ inch thickness. Stir together jelly, vinegar, mustard and salt. Coat broiling pan or outdoor grill with oil or nonstick cooking spray. Brush chicken breasts with sauce and broil or grill over high heat for 4 to 5 minutes on each side, or until done. Makes 6 servings.

BACON-WRAPPED CHICKEN

6	**boneless, skinless chicken breasts**
$1/2$ cup	**finely diced green onions**
I package (8 ounces)	**cream cheese,** softened
12 strips	**uncooked bacon**

Preheat oven to 350 degrees.

Place chicken between two pieces of plastic wrap and pound to an even thickness, about $1/2$ inch thick. Stir green onions into cream cheese. Spread about 3 tablespoons cream cheese mixture onto one side of each flattened chicken breast. Roll up jelly-roll style. Wrap each chicken roll with two pieces of bacon, covering entire surface of chicken. Place chicken rolls in a 9 x 13-inch baking pan, seam side down. Bake, uncovered, for 60 minutes. Just before serving, broil for a few minutes until bacon is crispy and browned. Makes 6 servings.

CHICKEN CORDON BLEU

6	**boneless, skinless chicken breasts**
6 thick slices	**Swiss cheese**
6 thick slices	**ham**
I cup	**flour**
2	**eggs,** slightly beaten
I cup	**seasoned breadcrumbs**
	Oil for sauteing

Lay chicken breast on cutting board with widest side flat on board. Make a slit lengthwise, parallel to cutting board, into each breast, creating a large pocket. Insert cheese and ham into each breast pocket. Coat each breast thoroughly with flour first, then dip each breast into egg, coating evenly. Coat each breast with breadcrumbs. Heat $1/4$ inch of oil in a saute pan. Cook breasts over medium heat two at a time for 5–8 minutes on each side, or until cooked through. Makes 6 servings.

CRANBERRY CHICKEN AND RICE

1 can (16 ounces)	**whole cranberry sauce**
1 cup	**Russian salad dressing**
$1/4$ cup	**orange juice concentrate**
2 to 3 pounds	**boneless, skinless chicken pieces**
8 cups	**cooked rice**

Preheat oven to 350 degrees.

In a bowl, combine cranberry sauce, Russian dressing and orange juice concentrate. Pour half the mixture into a 9 x 13-inch baking pan. Place chicken in pan in a single layer. Pour remaining sauce over chicken pieces. Cover and refrigerate at least 2 hours or overnight. Remove from refrigerator, uncover and bring to room temperature, about 20 minutes. Bake for 80–90 minutes, basting occasionally. Serve over warm rice. Makes 6–8 servings.

ONION-BAKED CHICKEN

2 to 3 pounds	**boneless, skinless chicken breast tenderloins**
I envelope	**dry onion soup mix**
3 tablespoons	**butter or margarine,** melted
I	**yellow onion,** thinly sliced

Preheat oven to 350 degrees.

Place chicken and dry onion soup mix in a gallon-size ziplock bag. Shake to evenly coat chicken soup mix. Place chicken in bottom of 9 x 13-inch or larger baking pan. Drizzle melted butter evenly over chicken tenders. Layer sliced onion evenly over chicken. Bake 35 minutes, or until chicken is no longer pink. Once done, break apart chicken tenders and serve with the baked onions on top. Serve with seasoned mashed potatoes and a green salad on the side. Makes 6–8 servings.

MUSHROOM-STUFFED CHICKEN BREASTS

6	**boneless, skinless chicken breasts**
8 ounces	**sliced mushrooms**
2 tablespoons	**butter**
4 tablespoons	**cream cheese,** softened
1 teaspoon	**garlic salt**
$^1/_2$ cup	**water**
1 can (10 ounces)	**golden mushroom soup,** condensed

Preheat oven to 400 degrees.

Lay chicken breasts with widest side down on a cutting board. Make a large slit in widest portion of breast to form a pocket. Saute mushrooms in butter 3 to 5 minutes, or until mushrooms are soft and most of liquid has evaporated. Stir in cream cheese and garlic salt. Stuff chicken breasts with mixture. Place breasts in a 9 x 13-inch baking pan. Stir water into soup and spread on top of each breast. Bake for 40–50 minutes, or until browned and cooked through. Let stand 5 minutes before serving. Makes 6 servings.

PECAN-CRUSTED CHICKEN BREASTS

6	**boneless, skinless chicken breasts**
2 cups	**brown sugar**
1 cup	**Dijon mustard**
1 teaspoon	**salt**
1 1/2 cups	**finely crushed pecans**

Preheat oven to 400 degrees.

Lay each chicken breast with the widest side down on a cutting board. With a large sharp knife parallel to the cutting surface, slice off a small portion of the chicken breast so that it is a uniform thickness, about 1/2 inch thick. Save the small removed portions of chicken for another use. Mix brown sugar, mustard and salt in a small bowl. Coat chicken pieces with mixture. Spread crushed pecans on a small plate and then roll coated chicken in pecans and press firmly. Place coated breasts in a 9 x 13-inch baking pan and bake for 40 minutes. Let stand 5 minutes before serving. Makes 6 servings.

VARIATION: Use crushed walnuts, hazelnuts or pistachios instead of pecans for a different flavor.

SWEET HAWAIIAN CHICKEN

3 to 4 pounds	**boneless, skinless chicken pieces**
1 can (20 ounces)	**pineapple rings,** drained and juice reserved
1 1/2 cups	**teriyaki sauce**
1/2 cup	**brown sugar**
1/4 cup	**soy sauce**
2 tablespoons	**Worcestershire sauce**
2 tablespoons	**cornstarch,** mixed with 1/4 cup water

Preheat oven to 350 degrees.

Chop chicken into large chunks and place in a gallon-size ziplock bag. Mix together 3/4 cup pineapple juice, teriyaki sauce, brown sugar, soy sauce and Worcestershire sauce. Pour sauce into bag and refrigerate 2 hours or more. (The longer the marinating time, the more the chicken will absorb the sauce.) Remove chicken from refrigerator and drain most of the liquid into a small saucepan. Add cornstarch and water mixture. Bring to a low boil for 2–3 minutes, or until thickened. Spread chicken in a 9 x 13-inch baking pan and then bake 40 minutes, covered. Dip pineapple rings in sauce. Remove chicken from oven and top with pineapple rings. Bake, uncovered, for 20 minutes more, broiling the last few minutes to brown the pineapple rings. Serve over warm rice, if desired. Serves 6 to 8.

CHICKEN AND YAM BAKE

8 **boneless, skinless chicken thighs**
2 tablespoons **butter**
2 cans (29 ounces each) **yams in syrup,** drained and $1/4$ cup
syrup reserved
$1/2$ cup **raisins**
1 can (12 ounces) **evaporated milk**
2 teaspoons **salt**
2 tablespoons **cornstarch**
$1/4$ teaspoon **ground nutmeg**
$1/4$ teaspoon **cinnamon**

Preheat oven to 350 degrees.

Cut chicken into small cubes, $1/2$ to 1 inch diameter. Saute chicken in
butter over medium-high heat until well done and browned, stirring
occasionally, for 12–15 minutes. Mix drained yams, raisins and chicken
and spread in a 9 x 13-inch baking pan. Mix reserved syrup, evaporated
milk, salt, cornstarch and spices. Pour over chicken mixture. Bake for
1 hour and then let stand 5 minutes before serving. Makes 8–10 servings.

INTERNATIONAL ENTREES

TANDOORI CHICKEN

8	**skinless chicken thighs**
$^1/_3$ cup	**lemon juice**
$^1/_2$	**yellow onion**
6	**cloves garlic**
I tablespoon	**minced ginger**
I tablespoon	**cumin**
I tablespoon	**paprika**
I teaspoon	**salt**
I cup	**plain yogurt**
a few drops	**red food coloring** (optional)

Preheat oven to 350 degrees.

Place chicken and lemon juice in a gallon-size ziplock bag. Seal and refrigerate 1–2 hours. Blend remaining ingredients in a food processor or blender until smooth. Brush chicken with mixture and place in and 8 x 8-inch pan. Pour remaining yogurt mixture over chicken. Refrigerate overnight. Remove chicken from refrigerator and bring to room temperature, about 20 minutes. Bake for 50–60 minutes, or until cooked through. Makes 4–6 servings.

CHICKEN SATAY
WITH PEANUT SAUCE

3	**boneless, skinless chicken breasts**
3 tablespoons	**soy sauce,** divided
3 tablespoons	**lemon juice,** divided
3	**cloves minced fresh garlic**
1 tablespoon	**sesame oil**
1 teaspoon	**curry powder**
$^1/_2$ cup	**natural peanut butter**
1 cup	**canned coconut milk**
$^1/_4$ cup	**brown sugar**
$^1/_4$ teaspoon	**cayenne pepper,** or more to taste

Cut chicken breasts into flat strips about 1 x 2 inches (about 30 pieces total). Place chicken in a large ziplock bag. Mix 2 tablespoons soy sauce, 2 tablespoons lemon juice, garlic and oil together. Pour into bag and seal. Set aside on counter to marinate at room temperature for 30 minutes, turning bag over frequently. Combine all remaining ingredients in a small bowl to make sauce and then set aside; warm when ready to use. Thread marinated chicken pieces onto skewers so that cubes of chicken are barely touching. Broil on high heat in oven for about 5 minutes, or grill on outdoor grill, watching closely. Turn skewers over. Broil or grill another 3–5 minutes, or until lightly browned. Serve warm with rice and peanut sauce. Makes 4–6 servings.

PASTEL DE CHOCLO

1 cup	**milk**
2 packages (16 ounces each)	**frozen corn,** thawed
1 tablespoon	**basil**
4 teaspoons	**sugar,** divided
1/2 teaspoon	**salt**
1/2 teaspoon	**black pepper**
1 1/2 teaspoons	**cornstarch**
1 can (14 ounces)	**chicken broth**
1	**large onion,** chopped
2 to 3	**boneless, skinless chicken breasts**

Preheat oven to 400 degrees.

In a blender or food processor, blend milk, corn, and basil together until smooth. In a large pan, bring corn mixture to a boil, stirring constantly. Reduce heat and simmer 15 minutes. Remove from heat and stir in 1 teaspoon sugar, salt, black pepper and cornstarch. Set mixture aside.

In a separate pan, bring broth, onion, and chicken to a boil. Reduce heat, cover, and simmer for 20 minutes, or until chicken is done. Drain chicken and onion mixture and then place in bottom of a greased 8 x 8-inch or 9 x 9-inch pan. Spread corn mixture over top. Sprinkle with remaining sugar. Bake for 25 minutes and then broil for 2–3 minutes to lightly brown the top. Serve with diced fresh tomatoes. Makes 4 servings.

CANJA CHICKEN SOUP

2	**boneless, skinless chicken breasts**
8 cups	**chicken broth**
I	**large onion,** chopped
3	**carrots,** peeled and sliced
2 tablespoons	**dried mint leaves**
I	**large tomato,** diced
I cup	**diced cooked ham**
8 cups	**cooked rice**
I cup	**minced fresh parsley**

Dice chicken into bite-sized pieces, removing visible fat. Bring chicken, broth, and onion to a boil and then cover and simmer slowly for 30 minutes. Add carrots and dried mint leaves and then simmer another 20 minutes. Add tomato and ham and simmer 10 minutes more. Ladle soup into 8 individual shallow serving bowls. Spray a 1-cup sized dish or measuring cup with nonstick cooking spray. Press 1 cup of rice firmly into cup, compacting rice to about $^3/_4$ cup. Invert pressed rice into center of soup bowl so that mounded rice is sticking up higher than soup. Repeat for each soup bowl. Sprinkle with a little parsley to garnish and serve warm. Makes 8 servings.

KELAGUEN

1 (2–2$^1/_2$ pound)	**cooked rotisserie chicken**
1$^1/_2$ cups	**unsweetened grated coconut**
$^1/_2$ cup	**chopped green onions**
2 to 3 tablespoons	**crushed red pepper**
1 or 2	**lemons,** juiced
	salt

Remove meat from bones and finely chop; discard bones and skin. In a large bowl, combine coconut, onion, crushed pepper and lemon juice. Sprinkle mixture evenly over chicken and then salt to taste. Serve with warm tortillas or crackers. Makes 4–6 servings.

CHICKEN ENCHILADA STACKS

2 cans (19 ounces each)	**enchilada sauce**
1 can (14.5 ounces)	**stewed tomatoes,** drained
18	**corn tortillas**
3	**boneless, skinless chicken breasts,** cooked and diced
1 envelope	**taco seasoning**
4 cups	**grated sharp cheddar cheese**
1 can (7 ounces)	**diced green chiles**

Pour enchilada sauce and tomatoes in a blender and blend until smooth. Pour into a medium saucepan and bring to a simmer. Using a small frying pan, heat to medium heat. Cook each tortilla about 20 seconds, turning frequently, or until cooked through but not crisp. Toss chicken with taco seasoning and then set aside. To assemble each stack, layer on a microwaveable plate for each person according to the following. Dip a tortilla in pan of sauce and then place on a plate. Spread with $^1/_2$ cup cheese. Place another dipped tortilla on top of cheese and then sprinkle with $^1/_2$ cup chicken. Place another dipped tortilla on top and then sprinkle with a scant tablespoon of green chiles and 1 tablespoon cheese. Microwave each stack for 90 seconds and then serve immediately. Makes 6 servings.

POMEGRANATE CHICKEN

1 (3- to 4-pound) **whole chicken,** cut up
1/4 cup **olive oil**
1 teaspoon **garlic powder**
8 ounces **pomegranate juice**
1/2 cup **apple juice**
3 tablespoons **sugar**
2 teaspoons **cinnamon**
1 teaspoon **salt**

Preheat oven to 375 degrees.

Cut breast pieces in half and then brush all chicken pieces with oil and sprinkle with garlic powder. Arrange chicken in a 9 x13-inch baking pan and bake for 30 minutes. Meanwhile, stir remaining ingredients together in a small saucepan and simmer until reduced by half. Remove chicken from oven and carefully remove skin with a fork. Pierce chicken with fork multiple times. Brush chicken generously on both sides with liquid. Return to oven and cook another 30 minutes. Remove from oven, pour remaining liquid over chicken and let sit 5 to 10 minutes before serving. Makes 4–6 servings.

MEDITERRANEAN CHICKEN

1 (3- to 4-pound)	**whole chicken,** cut up
2 tablespoons	**seasoned salt**
1 jar (5 ounces)	**kalamata or regular olives,** drained, rinsed and sliced
1 can (14 ounces)	**diced tomatoes with onion and garlic,** undrained
1 jar (6 ounces)	**artichoke hearts,** undrained
6 ounces	**crumbled feta cheese**

Preheat oven to 350 degrees.

Season chicken pieces with seasoned salt and place in a 9 x 13-inch baking pan. Bake for 1 hour. Place olives, tomatoes and artichoke hearts in a small saucepan and simmer 15–20 minutes, stirring occasionally, or until liquid has reduced by half. Remove chicken from oven and carefully remove the skin. Pour mixture over chicken and let stand 10 minutes. Sprinkle feta cheese on top and serve. Makes 4–6 servings.

CHICKEN ITALIANO

4	**boneless, skinless chicken breasts**
I cup	**cornstarch**
3	**eggs,** slightly beaten
I cup	**breadcrumbs**
$^{1}/_{2}$ cup	**grated Parmesan cheese**
$^{1}/_{2}$ cup	**canola oil**
I jar (26 ounces)	**spaghetti sauce**
4 slices	**prosciutto or Italian sausage**
4 slices	**fresh mozzarella**

Place chicken breasts between two sheets of plastic wrap and flatten
to uniform thickness, about $^{1}/_{2}$ inch. Dredge chicken first in cornstarch,
then in egg and then in breadcrumb mixed with Parmesan cheese.
Refrigerate for 15–20 minutes so coating will set. Heat oil in skillet to
medium high heat. Place chicken pieces in skillet and cook 8–10 minutes on first side, checking frequently to prevent burning. Turn pieces
over and cook another 6–8 minutes, or until chicken is cooked
through. Remove chicken from skillet and then pour sauce into skillet
and bring to a simmer. Meanwhile, place prosciutto and cheese on top
of each chicken breast. Return chicken stacks to skillet and cover.
Reduce heat to low and cook another 3–5 minutes to heat through.
Makes 4 servings.

30-MINUTE PAELLA

3 slices	**bacon,** finely diced
2	**boneless, skinless chicken breasts,** cooked and diced
1/2 each	**green and red bell pepper,** diced
1 large	**onion,** diced
2 cups	**uncooked minute rice**
2 cups	**water**
1 teaspoon	**turmeric**
1 teaspoon	**salt**
16 ounces	**cooked tiny shrimp**
1 cup	**frozen peas**

Cook bacon in a large skillet or wok over high heat until browned, about 2 minutes, and then remove. Saute chicken for 3 minutes, then add bell peppers and onion and cook for another 5 minutes. Stir in rice, water, turmeric and salt. Cover and reduce to a simmer for 10 minutes. Add shrimp and peas and simmer, uncovered, 10 minutes more, or until liquid is evaporated. Makes 6–8 servings.

ASIAN LETTUCE WRAPS

3	**boneless, skinless chicken breasts,** diced
2 tablespoons	**cornstarch**
I tablespoon	**grated fresh ginger**
$1/2$ cup	**roasted garlic teriyaki marinade**
$1/4$ cup	**canola oil**
I tablespoon	**sesame oil**
I cup	**diced celery**
2 cans (8 ounces each)	**sliced water chestnuts,** drained and chopped
$1/2$ head	**iceberg lettuce**

Place chicken in a small bowl. Stir cornstarch and ginger into teriyaki marinade. Stir sauce into chicken and let stand at room temperature for 20–30 minutes. Heat oils in a large skillet or wok. Add chicken and saute 3–5 minutes, or until chicken is cooked through. Stir in the diced celery and water chestnuts. Serve in a large bowl, with a $1/2$ head of iceberg lettuce on a plate. Each guest places a few tablespoons of chicken mixture in a lettuce leaf and then rolls up jelly-roll style before eating. Makes 6–8 servings.

CHICKEN YAKISOBA

2	**boneless, skinless chicken breasts,** diced
1 tablespoon	**cornstarch**
$3/4$ cup	**teriyaki marinade**
$1/4$ cup	**canola oil**
2 tablespoons	**sesame oil**
2 cups	**diced vegetables,** such as carrots, celery, pea pods, green onions and red bell peppers
2 packages (8 ounces each)	**refrigerated Yakisoba stir-fry noodles**

Place chicken in a small bowl. Stir cornstarch into teriyaki marinade and pour half the mixture into chicken. Let sit for 20–30 minutes, or until chicken comes to room temperature. Heat oils in a large skillet or wok. Saute chicken 3–5 minutes, or until cooked through. Add vegetables and noodles and then cook 3 minutes more. Add remaining teriyaki sauce and cook another 5–6 minutes, or until sauce thickens. Makes 4–6 servings.

JAMAICAN JERK SALAD

4	**boneless, skinless chicken breasts**
4 tablespoons	**canola oil**
4 tablespoons	**jerk seasoning***
1 bag (16 ounces)	**salad greens mix**
1 cup	**honey mustard salad dressing**
1/4 cup	**lime juice**
2	**fresh mangos,** thinly sliced

Place chicken breasts on a cutting surface, widest side down. With a large knife parallel to cutting surface, slice breast into two wide flat planks, about 1/4 to 1/2 inch thick. Brush oil on chicken and then sprinkle with jerk seasoning. Broil or grill chicken for 3–5 minutes. Turn, brush oil over surface, and then season again. Broil or grill again until cooked through and lightly browned. Remove from oven and slice chicken in long, thin strips. Toss greens with dressing mixed with lime juice, reserving 2 tablespoons of dressing for garnish. Spread some greens on a serving plate. Arrange mango and chicken slices on top. Drizzle with remaining dressing. Makes 4–6 servings.

*If seasoning is not available at the grocery store, mix 2 teaspoons onion powder, 1 teaspoon sugar, 1 teaspoon chili powder, 1 teaspoon thyme, 1 teaspoon salt, 1/2 teaspoon ground cloves and 1/2 teaspoon ground cinnamon together in a small bowl.

CHICKEN STROGANOFF

3	**boneless, skinless chicken breasts**
1/4 cup	**butter**
1 large	**onion,** julienned
8 ounces	**sliced mushrooms**
1 cup	**sour cream**
1 teaspoon	**Dijon mustard**
2 tablespoons	**tomato paste**
1/4 cup	**ketchup**
1 tablespoon	**Worcestershire sauce**
8 cups	**cooked rice or egg noodles**

Slice chicken lengthwise into thin strips and saute in butter in a large skillet or wok until cooked through. Stir onion and mushrooms into skillet. Cook until onions are limp and then add sour cream, mustard, tomato paste and Worcestershire sauce. Cook 10–12 minutes, or until sauce has thickened, stirring constantly. Serves over rice or noodles. Makes 6–8 servings.

CHICKEN CURRY

1 can (14 ounces)	**coconut milk**
2 tablespoons	**green or red curry paste,** or more to taste
2 to 3	**boneless, skinless chicken breasts**
2 tablespoons	**brown sugar**
2 cans (8 ounces each)	**sliced bamboo shoots**
1 cup	**frozen peas**
	cooked rice

In a large skillet, bring coconut milk and curry paste to a simmer. Cut chicken into bite-size pieces and add to skillet. Simmer for 10 minutes, stirring frequently. Add remaining ingredients except rice and simmer another 10–15 minutes, stirring frequently, or until sauce thickens. Serve over cooked rice. Makes 6 servings.

Family Favorites

BBQ CHICKEN PIZZA

1 tube (13.8 ounces) **refrigerated pizza crust dough**
$^1/_2$ cup **barbecue sauce**
1 can (10–13 ounces) **chunk chicken breast,** drained
$^1/_2$ **medium red onion,** thinly sliced
1$^1/_2$ cups **grated mozzarella or Italian-blend cheese**

Preheat oven to 400 degrees.

Press dough to cover a greased baking sheet and bake 8 minutes. Spread barbecue sauce over crust and then layer with chicken, red onion, and cheese. Bake 6–10 minutes more, or until crust bottom is light golden brown. Makes 6–8 servings.

CHICKEN ALFREDO PIZZA

I tube (13.8 ounces)	**refrigerated pizza crust dough**
I jar (16 ounces)	**alfredo sauce**
I can (10–13 ounces)	**chunk chicken breast,** drained*
I	**red bell pepper,** seeded and chopped
1/4 cup	**chopped green onion**
1 1/2 cups	**mozzarella cheese**

Preheat oven to 400 degrees.

Press dough to cover a greased baking sheet and bake 8 minutes. Remove from oven and spread three-fourths of the alfredo sauce over crust. Top evenly with chicken, bell pepper, green onion, and cheese. Bake 6–10 minutes more, or until crust bottom is light golden brown. Serve with remaining alfredo sauce for dipping. Makes 6–8 servings.

*1 1/2 cups cooked white chicken breast meat may be substituted.

BREADED CHICKEN NUGGETS

4 to 5 **boneless, skinless chicken breasts**
I cup **seasoned Italian breadcrumbs**
$^1/_2$ cup **grated Parmesan cheese**
$^1/_2$ teaspoon **salt**
I $^1/_2$ teaspoons **paprika**
$^1/_2$ cup **butter,** melted

Preheat oven to 400 degrees.

In a bowl, combine breadcrumbs, cheese, salt and paprika. Dip chicken pieces into melted butter, then roll in crumb mixture, heavily coating chicken. Place pieces evenly on bottom of a large baking sheet. Bake 20–25 minutes, or until crispy and done. Serve with ranch dressing or ketchup on the side. Makes 4 servings.

OVEN-FRIED
BUTTERMILK CHICKEN

1 cup	**dry breadcrumbs**
$^1/_3$ cup	**grated Parmesan cheese**
1 teaspoon	**garlic salt**
1 (4- to 5-pound)	**whole chicken,** cut up
$^1/_2$ cup	**cornstarch**
1 cup	**buttermilk**

Preheat oven to 375 degrees.

Combine breadcrumbs, cheese and garlic salt and spread on a plate.
Rinse chicken pieces and pat dry. Sprinkle cornstarch onto chicken
pieces to evenly coat with a fine dusting. Carefully dip chicken pieces
in buttermilk and then dredge in crumb mixture. Place chicken in a
9 x 13-inch baking pan so pieces are not touching. Place in refrigerator
for 20 minutes so coating mixture sets. Remove from refrigerator and
place a wire baking rack on top of a jelly roll pan or other large baking
sheet. Place chicken pieces on top of wire rack and bake for 50–60
minutes, or until chicken is cooked through and coating is browned.
Makes 4–6 servings.

PARMESAN-CRUSTED DRUMSTICKS

1 cup	**seasoned breadcrumbs**
2/3 cup	**grated Parmesan cheese**
1 teaspoon	**minced garlic**
1 tablespoon	**parsley**
8	**chicken drumsticks**
1/3 cup	**butter,** melted

Preheat oven to 375 degrees.

In a bowl, combine breadcrumbs, cheese, garlic, and parsley. Dip drumsticks in butter, then coat in crumb mixture. Place chicken skin side up on a greased baking sheet with sides. Bake 50 minutes, or until crisp and tender. Makes 6–8 servings.

FAMILY FIESTA CASSEROLE

3 cups	**cooked, cubed chicken**
2 cans (15 ounces each)	**black beans,** drained
2 cups	**frozen corn**
I can (4 ounces)	**diced green chiles**
I cup	**medium hot salsa**
I cup	**sour cream**
6 cups	**crushed corn chips,** such as Fritos
4 cups	**grated pepper jack cheese**

Preheat oven to 350 degrees.

Mix chicken, beans, corn, chiles, salsa and sour cream. Spread half the corn chips in a 9 x 13-inch baking pan. Spread half the chicken mixture on top. Sprinkle half the cheese over top and then repeat layers. Bake 30–40 minutes, or until cooked through and bubbly on top. Makes 6–8 servings.

ONE-DISH SUNDAY SUPPER

2 large **red onions**
8 to 10 **red potatoes,** about 3 pounds
3 pounds **boneless, skinless chicken thighs**
1 bag (16 ounces) **baby carrots**
2 cans (10 ounces each) **golden mushroom soup,** condensed
1 cup **sour cream**

Preheat oven to 350 degrees.

Cut onions and potatoes into 2-inch cubes. Arrange chicken, potatoes, carrots and onion in a large 3-quart baking pan. Combine soup and sour cream and then pour over top. Bake, covered, for 30 minutes. Remove from oven, stir and cook 30 minutes more, uncovered. Makes 6–8 servings.

CHICKEN FAJITA QUESADILLAS

2 tablespoons	**olive oil**
I pound	**boneless, skinless chicken breasts,** cubed
I envelope	**fajita seasoning mix**
2 tablespoons	**water**
I	**red bell pepper,** seeded and cut into bite size pieces
2	**green bell peppers,** seeded and cut into bite size pieces
I	**red onion,** thinly sliced
10	**burrito-size flour tortillas**
I $^1/_2$ cups	**grated cheddar cheese**
I $^1/_2$ cups	**grated Mexican-blend cheese**

Preheat oven to 350 degrees.

In a large saucepan, heat oil. Stir in cubed chicken. Cook chicken until no longer pink, stirring frequently. Add fajita seasoning, water, bell peppers and onion to saucepan. Cook 7–8 minutes, or until vegetables are tender. Layer half of each tortilla with cheddar cheese, chicken mixture and then Mexican cheese. Fold tortilla in half over meat and cheese. Bake quesadillas 8–10 minutes on baking sheets, or until cheese melts. Makes 8–10 servings.

EASY CHICKEN PICATTA

4	**boneless, skinless chicken breasts**
2 tablespoons	**canola oil**
I tablespoon	**butter**
I cup	**cornstarch**
$^1/_2$ cup	**apple juice**
I cup	**chicken broth**
I whole	**lemon,** thinly sliced
$^1/_4$ cup	**chopped parsley**
3 tablespoons	**capers** (optional)
I cup	**sliced green onions**

Lay chicken flat and, with a large, sharp knife parallel to cutting surface, cut each breast into two large flat planks. Heat oil and butter in a large saute pan. Coat chicken with cornstarch and saute a few pieces at a time, about 2 minutes on each side, or until lightly browned. Remove and set aside. Add the juice and broth to the pan and scrape with a wooden spoon to deglaze pan. Add lemon slices, parsley, capers (if desired) and onions to pan and cook over medium-high heat for 3–5 minutes, or until onions are limp. Remove lemon slices and reserve for garnish. Slice cooked chicken pieces into $^1/_2$-inch-wide slices and add to pan. Cook another 2–3 minutes, or until chicken is heated through. Top with lemon slices as a garnish. Makes 4–6 servings.

CHICKEN BROCCOLI CASSEROLE

3 cups **cooked rice**
4 cups **coarsely chopped broccoli**
4 **boneless, skinless chicken breasts,** cooked and cubed
1 cup **grated cheddar cheese**
2 cans (10 ounces each) **cream of chicken soup,** condensed
$^1/_2$ cup **sour cream**
1 tablespoon **lemon juice**
1 teaspoon **curry powder** (optional)

Preheat oven to 350 degrees.

Spread rice in the bottom of a 9 x 13-inch baking pan sprayed with nonstick cooking spray. Place broccoli over rice and then chicken over broccoli. Stir together remaining ingredients and pour over top. Bake for 35–40 minutes. Makes 6–8 servings.

RANCH-SEASONED CHICKEN

4 **boneless, skinless chicken breasts**
1 envelope **ranch dressing mix**
$^1/_4$ cup **breadcrumbs**

Preheat oven to 375 degrees.

Combine dressing mix and breadcrumbs in a large ziplock bag. Add chicken to bag and shake until coated. Place chicken in a greased 9 x 13-inch pan. Bake for 25–30 minutes, or until chicken is done. Makes 4 servings.

CHICKEN POTPIE

I bag (16 ounces) **frozen stew vegetables,** thawed
I small box (8 ounces) **frozen peas**
I can (6 ounces) **mushroom pieces,** drained
2 **boneless, skinless chicken breasts,** cooked and cubed
2 cans (10 ounces each) **chicken and mushroom soup,** condensed
I sheet (8.5 ounces) **frozen puff pastry,** thawed

Preheat oven to 350 degrees.

Cut any large pieces of stew vegetables into bite-size pieces. Stir together vegetables, peas, mushrooms, chicken and soup and then spoon into a 2-quart rectangular baking dish. Cut sheet of puff pastry to fit dish and place on top. Cut slits in pastry about 2 inches apart and bake for 45–50 minutes, or until mixture is bubbly and pastry is lightly browned. Makes 6–8 servings.

CHICKEN AND SAUSAGE CASSOULET

1 bag (16 ounces)	**white beans**
1 can (6 ounces)	**tomato paste**
1 can (14 ounces)	**diced tomatoes**
2 cans (14 ounces each)	**chicken broth**
1 cup	**apple cider**
6 slices	**bacon,** diced
2 pounds	**boneless, skinless chicken breasts**
1 ring (16 ounces)	**sausage**
6 cloves	**garlic,** diced
1 small bag (12 ounces)	**baby carrots**

Place beans in a pan and cover with water overnight; drain and rinse. In a 5- to 7-quart slow cooker, stir tomato paste, tomatoes, broth and cider together. Cook bacon in a small skillet until crisp. Cut chicken into pieces the size of a deck of cards. Cut sausage into 2-inch pieces. Stir all ingredients together in slow cooker and cook 6–8 hours on high heat. Makes 8–10 servings.

MUSHROOM AND ARTICHOKE CHICKEN

4	**boneless, skinless chicken breasts,** cooked and cubed
1 can or jar (14 ounces)	**artichoke hearts in oil,** drained and chopped
2 cans (4 ounces each)	**sliced mushrooms,** drained
1 jar (16 ounces)	**alfredo sauce,** any variety
1 cup	**sliced toasted almonds**
8 cups	**cooked rice**

Preheat oven to 350 degrees.

Combine chicken and artichoke hearts. Place in a 9 x 13-inch baking pan. Add the mushrooms and then pour the alfredo sauce over top. Bake for 30–40 minutes, or until cooked through and bubbly around the edges. Sprinkle with sliced almonds and serve over rice. Makes 6–8 servings.

SALSA CHICKEN

4 to 5 **boneless, skinless chicken breasts**
1 envelope **taco seasoning**
1 jar (16 ounces) **chunky salsa**
1 cup **grated cheddar cheese**
sour cream

Preheat oven to 375 degrees.

Place chicken in a greased 9 x 13-inch pan. Sprinkle taco seasoning on both sides of each breast. Pour salsa over chicken and then bake for 30–35 minutes, or until chicken is done. Sprinkle cheese over chicken and then bake 5 minutes more, or until cheese melts. Garnish with sour cream, if desired. Makes 4–5 servings.

CHICKEN AND RICE CASSEROLE

3	**boneless, skinless chicken breasts**
2 tablespoons	**butter**
2 cups	**uncooked rice**
2 cups	**water,** divided
1 tablespoon	**lemon juice**
1 teaspoon	**salt**
3 cups	**sliced mushrooms**
1 teaspoon	**Worcestershire sauce**
1 can (10 ounces)	**cream of mushroom soup,** condensed

Preheat oven to 350 degrees.

Slice each chicken breast in half to make two flat planks. Saute in butter until cooked through. Generously spray a 9 x 13-inch baking pan with nonstick cooking spray. Spread rice in pan. Mix 1 cup of water, lemon juice and salt together and pour over rice. Spread mushrooms on top of rice. Mix remaining water, Worcestershire sauce and soup together. Pour half of soup mixture over mushrooms. Place chicken pieces on top, covering entire surface and then pour remaining soup mixture over chicken. Cover and bake for 40 minutes. Uncover and cook 10 minutes more. Makes 6 servings.

SOUTHWEST VARIATION: Replace mushrooms with chopped green and red bell peppers. Use southwest style pepper jack soup instead of mushroom.

GARDEN VEGETABLE VARIATION: Replace mushrooms with chopped celery, carrots and onion. Use cream of celery soup instead of mushroom.

CHICKEN PASTRY PACKETS

1 box (17.5 ounces)	**frozen puff pastry**
4	**boneless, skinless chicken breasts**
2 tablespoons	**butter**
1 container (6.5 ounces)	**garlic and herb soft-cheese spread**
8 teaspoons	**dried parsley flakes**
1	**egg white,** whisked with 1 tablespoon water

Preheat oven to 400 degrees.

Unfold and thaw 2 puff pastry sheets on wax paper. Cut each sheet into 4 squares, making 8 squares total. Cut each chicken breast into two planks, each about the size of a deck of cards. Reserve scraps for another use. Saute chicken over medium-high heat in butter until lightly browned, about 2 minutes on each side. Remove from pan and let cool to room temperature. Spread center of each pastry square with 1 tablespoon cheese spread, leaving $1/2$ inch around the edges of each square. Sprinkle 1 teaspoon dried parsley flakes over cheese. Place a chicken piece on top of parsley and then spread 1 teaspoon cheese on top of each chicken piece. With a pastry brush, brush edges of each pastry square generously with egg mixture. Stretching gently, bring each corner of each pastry square up over chicken. Pinch center and all four seams tightly together. Place on baking sheet and bake 20–25 minutes, or until golden brown. Makes 8 servings.

GRANDMA DIRCKS' CHICKEN CASSEROLE

1 box (6 ounces)	**chicken stuffing mix,** divided
1 can (14.5 ounces)	**chicken broth,** divided
3 to 4	**boneless, skinless chicken breasts,** cooked and cubed
8 ounces	**sour cream**
1 can (10.5 ounces)	**cream of chicken soup,** condensed

Preheat oven to 350 degrees.

Sprinkle half the stuffing mix over bottom of a greased 9 x 9-inch pan. Drizzle $1/2$ cup broth over stuffing. Combine chicken, sour cream, remaining broth, soup, and remaining stuffing. Spread mixture over stuffing. Bake covered for 25 minutes. Uncover and bake 5–10 minutes more, or until set. Makes 4–6 servings.

NOTES

NOTES

NOTES

NOTES

NOTES

Metric Conversion Chart

Liquid and Dry Measures

U.S.	Canadian	Australian
$1/4$ teaspoon	1 mL	1 ml
$1/2$ teaspoon	2 mL	2 ml
1 teaspoon	5 mL	5 ml
1 Tablespoon	15 mL	20 ml
$1/4$ cup	50 mL	60 ml
$1/3$ cup	75 mL	80 ml
$1/2$ cup	125 mL	125 ml
$2/3$ cup	150 mL	170 ml
$3/4$ cup	175 mL	190 ml
1 cup	250 mL	250 ml
1 quart	1 liter	1 litre

Temperature Conversion Chart

Fahrenheit	Celsius
250	120
275	140
300	150
325	160
350	180
375	190
400	200
425	220
450	230
475	240
500	260

ABOUT THE AUTHORS

Donna Kelly lives in Provo, Utah, otherwise known as "Happy Valley." She is a cooking fanatic and loves to take recipes and give them her own new and flavorful twist. Her greatest training as a cook comes from nearly three decades of cooking for the pickiest eaters ever—her children Katie, Amy, Matt, and Jake. She currently works as a child abuse prosecutor, and finds great job satisfaction in working with abused children and bringing perpetrators to justice.

Stephanie Ashcraft, author of the original *101 Things To Do With A Cake Mix*, was raised near Kirklin, Indiana. She received a bachelor's degree in family science and a teaching certificate from Brigham Young University. Since 1998, she has taught cooking classes based on the tips and meals in her cookbooks. She currently lives with her husband and children in Tucson, Arizona.